RECEIVING the oil of Divine Favour

Dr. D. k. Olukoya

RECEIVING THE OIL OF DIVINE FAVOUR

Dr Daniel Olukoya

Receiving the oil of Divine Favour
©2010.Dr Daniel Olukoya

A publication of
MOUNTAIN OF FIRE AND MIRACLES MINISTRIES
13, Olasimbo Street, off Olumo Road, Onike,
P. O. Box 2990, Sabo, Yaba, Lagos, Nigeria.

ISBN: 978-978-8424-98-7

All rights reserved. No portion of this book may be used without the written permission of the publisher. It is protected under the copyright laws.

For further information or permission contact:
Email: pasteurdanielolukoya_french@yahoo.fr
mfmhqworldwide@mountainoffire.org

Or visit our website: www.mountainoffire.org
http://mfmbiligualbooks4evangelism.blogspot.com/

Psalm 5:12 *"For thou, Lord, wilt bless the righteous; with favour wilt thou compass him as with a shield".*

1 Samuel 2:7-8: *"The Lord maketh poor, and maketh rich: he bringeth low, and lifteth up. He raiseth up the poor out of the dust, and lifteth up the beggar from the dunghill, to set them among princes, and to make them inherit the throne of glory: for the pillars of the earth are the Lord's and he hath set the world upon them. He will keep the feet of his saints, and the wicked shall be silent in darkness; for by strength shall no man prevail. The adversaries of the Lord shall be broken to pieces; out of heaven shall he thunder upon them: the Lord shall judge the ends of the earth; and he shall give strength unto his king, and exalt the horn of his anointed".*

From these texts, it is clear that promotion belongs to God and comes from Him. The first one shows that we have a part to play: we must be righteous, for God to bless us with favour and His favour upon us will serve as shield from the fiery darts of the enemy. The second text goes further to say that if a person is a servant and in the dunghill, God can lift him or her from that state, to place the person where Princes sit; that is he or she is now on the same level with those that people are looking up to.

If you are a First-born and you are not finding your feet, it means your promotion has been stolen or transferred and you must be ready to pray today. God is able to lift anybody or relegate.

Proverbs 12:2: *"A good man obtaineth favour of the Lord: but a man of wicked devices will He condemn".*

Divine favour is a thing that everyone needs; it can turn around any unfavourable or terrible situation. There is no amount of limitation that divine favour cannot remove. If you read through the Bible, you will find out that through divine favour, many people won battles, many became heroes, slaves became kings, captives became captors, and confirmed failure became successful, all these happened under the oil of favour. I pray that the oil of favour shall fall upon you today in the Name of Jesus. By divine favour beloved, you will win the willingness of God to help, protect, and bless you.

Anyone that is seeking complete victory needs the oil of favour. If you want satanic agents to be under your feet, you need the oil of divine favour. Even in times of temptation, when others are falling and the same powers want to pull you down, or you are already, staggering and are about to fall, divine favour will sustain you. A servant, who has received divine favour, will be treated with honour and respect; that kind of servant will enjoy the privileges of freedom. With the oil of favour on your head, breakthroughs come easily. Divine favour will open the doors that the enemy has closed against you; it will remove the obstacles on the way and make you a celebrity. With the oil of favour on your head, even if you are in a desert situation, it will turn to Paradise. It turns your mountains to lowlands; turns impossibility to possibility and your wish becomes God's command. When you have divine favour, you have the concentrated presence of God that can do all things for you. Without the oil of favour, tragedy can occur instantly and wipe the person out. I pray that the oil of favour shall come upon you today in the Name of Jesus.

A woman was travelling in a luxurious bus one day and some people wanted to ease themselves and the driver stopped. As they were coming back to their seats, a man told the woman that her old school mate wanted to see her at the back. She wondered who the person could be and hesitated. The man insisted and she obliged. As soon as she got to the back of the bus, they heard a loud noise; it was a trailer that ran into their bus. It was the area where the woman's original seat was that was affected. The person that sat on the seat next to hers can be said to have perished, not just died. Looking back at the situation, the woman could not really say that the man that came to call her was a passenger in the bus. She could not say also, if there was actually an old school mate that wanted to see her.

What that woman enjoyed, was divine favour that moved her from where she was seating, away from tragedy. When divine favour is upon your life, you will command respect; all the efforts of your enemies will come to naught. When divine favour is upon your life, you become a mystery and those around you will wonder. You will become a lamb amongst wolves, which the wolves cannot devour; you will become a spectacle, like grains of corn in a bottle, which the cock can only stare at, but cannot eat. The angels of God will keep watch over you. Divine favour will make you a wonder to your contemporaries.

With divine favour upon you, Balaam could come with seven rams and altars and any kind of thing against you, but will be defeated. With divine favour in your camp, there will always be the shout of the king. With divine favour, God will respect every sound you make and He backs it up. Divine favour will draw a mark around you and the enemy cannot touch it.

The key to an uncommon position, the key to being highly lifted, is divine favour. There are different kinds of oil. There are positive and negative oils. There are oils that will be upon your head and your cup will be filled and it will run over. There is oil that comes upon your head and you become a king, or priest or prophet. If the oil of favour is upon you, you will be the only one that will be singled out for an uncommon promotion. Even if there is only one seat to occupy and there are many candidates, you will be the one that will be chosen. It there is only one contract to be given out it will be you that will be chosen. If there is only one person to be blessed, the person will be you. You will be singled out for good things, you will be distinguished amongst many people and you will stand out of the crowd without being crushed. Favour will announce you wherever you go. It is important for you to pray the prayers I am suggesting below, with all the seriousness that you can gather.

When divine favour is upon you, heavens will open upon you, irrespective of your circumstances. You need to understand how to draw upon the oil of divine favour. When you begin to draw this oil, your destiny will be beautified and God will be glorified and you will move forward. The key to that promotion that you are seeking, is divine favour; the power of favour, which comes upon you and you will outshine other people; even those who have been on the queue before you.

Proverbs 22:1 *"A good name is rather to be chosen than great riches, and loving favour rather than silver and gold"*.

When you have favour, you do not have to bother about riches; they will come. If you must have uncommon success, you must have divine favour.

After a crusade abroad, a sister that attended got the oil of favour. She is a medical doctor and she applied for a job. She was the only African candidate. Out of the five examiners, only one gave her 95 %. The others gave her 98 % each. When she started working, she was in the midst of experts; elderly, experienced professors. They would go round the wards together, seeing patients. If there was a decision to be taken concerning a patient, the Professors would put heads together and would arrive at a conclusion. If she had any objection to their decision and suggested something else and they carried it out, the patient gets well faster than expected. Now, any time they go round the wards, even patients look out for her. She has since been promoted. All these happened, because she got the oil of divine favour.

The oil of favour could be stolen. An ordination from birth could be taken away, just as virtues could be transferred. That is why spiritual warfare is necessary, to possess that which you have lost, to capture back what the enemy has stolen and reposes that which is yours. Many people have never smelt that, which is theirs; the enemy never allowed them to see it, not to talk of possessing it. The prayers you are being asked to pray after reading through this message are prayers that were vomited by the Holy Ghost. I would like you to pray them with boiling anger. If you require fresh oil from the Lord, you shall receive it today in the Name of Jesus. If you desire uncommon promotion, pray them seriously. If you are a First-born and you are not finding your feet, make sure you pray like a mad prophet. The Angels of the Living God will pour upon your head, the anointing oil of favour. You would need to pray like blind

Bathemeus, who ran temporarily mad and cried out saying: *"Jesus, Son of David, have mercy on me"*.

People told him to shut up, but he shouted even louder.

A woman went to an Embassy for visa. Many people were turned down and she sat there, waiting. Suddenly, an indigene of that country working there walked up to her and asked her what she wanted. She said she wanted a visa, so that she could go to that country to buy shoes. The man asked if she had money and she said she did not, but that she wanted the visa, whilst trying to gather funds. The man asked her to give him her passport and come back at 2 pm to collect it with the visa on it. That was divine favour. She was singled out of the crowd. Normally, the fact that she did not have money for the business, should have disqualified her, but the oil of favour that made the man ask her questions, made him not to disqualify her for lack of funds.

This is a serious matter beloved, and I would like you to be serious about it. If hitherto, you have not surrendered your life to the Lord Jesus Christ, I would like you to take the decision to do it right away, right there where you are. You cannot receive the oil of favour from God, if you do not belong to Him. You have to leave the camp of the enemy and turn to the Lord. He is right there where you are and is ready to set you free from your sins and take you up in His arms. All you need do is acknowledge the fact that you are a sinner and that you cannot approach God in your sinful state. Repent of your sins; confess them to the Lord and ask Him to forgive you. Name them one by one, renounce and forsake them, and ask the Lord to cleanse you from all unrighteousness. Renounce the devil and the world of sin. Say bye-bye to them and make sure you do not go back to your vomit.

Open your heart and ask the Lord Jesus to come in. Invite Him into your life and ask Him to come in and become your personal Lord and Saviour. Enthrone Him over your life and ask Him to take absolute control of all that concerns you. Surrender your totality to Him and make Him the Lord of your life. I congratulate you for this decision that you have taken; I pray that it shall be permanent in your life in the Name of Jesus. I pray that your name shall be written in the Book of Life and nothing shall by any means, rub it off in the Name of Jesus. Go and sin no more!

Prayers

The kind of prayers that I am suggesting below, are the kind that many destinies have been waiting for. I would like to assure you that you have not read this message by chance and you shall not pray the prayers in vain, in the Name of Jesus.

1. Strongman stealing my favour, release it and die in the Name of Jesus.
2. Barriers to my favour, clear away in the Name of Jesus.
3. God arise and move me from labour to favour in the Name of Jesus.
4. Oil of favour, locate my head in the Name of Jesus.
5. My season of favour appear by fire in the Name of Jesus.
6. Every good thing that I have been looking for, begin to look for me now, in the Name of Jesus.

7. Every cloud of darkness around my destiny. Scatter in the Name of Jesus.
8. Every opposition shall become my gateway to testimonies in the Name of Jesus.
9. Every power, holding on to my favour, release it and die in the Name of Jesus.
10. Anointing for increasing greatness, fall upon my life now, in the Name of Jesus.
11. I revoke any conscious or unconscious covenant with the spirit of death, in the Name of Jesus.
12. Sudden death and untimely death will not be the lot of my family for ever, in the Name of Jesus.
13. I receive the power to fulfill my destiny, in the Name of Jesus.
14. Lord, release me from known and unknown curses, in the Name of Jesus.
15. Every mouth that has mocked me, shall congratulate me in the Name of Jesus.
16. I receive the perfume of divine favour in the Name of Jesus.

ABOUT D. K. OLUKOYA

Dr. D. K. Olukoya is the General Overseer of the Mountain of Fire and Miracles Ministries and the Battle Cry Ministries. He holds a First Class Honours Degree in Microbiology from the University of Lagos, Nigeria and a Ph.D. in Molecular Genetics from the University of Reading, United Kingdom. As a researcher, he has over eighty scientific publications to his credit. Anointed by God, Dr. Olukoya is a teacher, prophet, evangelist and preacher of the word. His life and that of his wife, Shade and their son, Elijah Toluwani, are living proofs that all power belongs to God.

1. A-Z of Complete Deliverance
2. Be Prepared
3. Bewitchment must die
4. Biblical Principles of Dream Interpretation
5. Born Great, But Tied Down
6. Breaking Bad Habits
7. Breakthrough Prayers For Business Professionals
8. Brokenness
9. Bringing Down The Power of God
10. Can God?
11. Can God Trust You?
12. Command The Morning
13. Consecration Commitment & Loyalty
14. Contending For The Kingdom
15. Connecting to The God of Breakthroughs
16. Criminals In The House Of God
17. Dealing With Hidden Curses
18. Dealing With Local Satanic Technology
19. Dealing With Satanic Exchange
20. Dealing With The Evil Powers Of Your Father's House
21. Dealing With Tropical Demons
22. Dealing With Unprofitable Roots
23. Dealing With Witchcraft Barbers
24. Deliverance By Fire
25. Deliverance From Spirit Husband And Spirit Wife
26. Deliverance From The Limiting Powers
27. Deliverance of The Brain
28. Deliverance Of The Conscience

29. Deliverance Of The Head
30. Deliverance: God's Medicine Bottle
31. Destiny Clinic
32. Destroying Satanic Masks
33. Disgracing Soul Hunters
34. Divine Military Training
35. Divine Yellow Card
36. Dominion Prosperity
37. Drawers Of Power From The Heavenlies
38. Evil Appetite
39. Evil Umbrella
40. Facing Both Ways
41. Failure In The School Of Prayer
42. Fire For Life's Journey
43. For We Wrestle ...
44. Freedom Indeed
45. Holiness Unto The Lord
46. Holy Cry
47. Holy Fever
48. Hour Of Decision
49. How To Obtain Personal Deliverance
50. How To Pray When Surrounded By The Enemies
51. Idols Of The Heart
52. Is This What They Died For?
53. Let God Answer By Fire
54. Limiting God
55. Madness Of The Heart
56. Making Your Way Through The Traffic Jam of Life

57. Meat For Champions
58. Medicine For Winners
59. My Burden For The Church
60. Open Heavens Through Holy Disturbance
61. Overpowering Witchcraft
62. Paralysing The Riders And The Horse
63. Personal Spiritual Check-Up
64. Power Against Coffin Spirits
65. Power Against Destiny Quenchers
66. Power Against Dream Criminals
67. Power Against Local Wickedness
68. Power Against Marine Spirits
69. Power Against Spiritual Terrorists
70. Power Must Change Hands
71. Pray Your Way To Breakthroughs
72. Prayer Is The Battle
73. Prayer Rain
74. Prayer Strategies For Spinsters And Bachelors
75. Prayer To Kill Enchantment
76. Prayer To Make You Fulfil Your Divine Destiny
77. Prayer Warfare Against 70 Mad Spirits
78. Prayers For Open Heavens
79. Prayers To Arrest Satanic Frustration
80. Prayers To Destroy Diseases And Infirmities
81. Prayers To Move From Minimum To Maximum
82. Praying Against The Spirit Of The Valley
83. Praying To Destroy Satanic Roadblocks
84. Praying To Dismantle Witchcraft

85. Principles Of Prayer
86. Release From Destructive Covenants
87. Revoking Evil Decrees
88. Safeguarding Your Home
89. Satanic Diversion Of The Black Race
90. Silencing The Birds Of Darkness
91. Slaves Who Love Their Chains
92. Smite The Enemy And He Will Flee
93. Speaking Destruction Unto The Dark Rivers
94. Spiritual Education
95. Spiritual Growth And Maturity
96. Spiritual Warfare And The Home
97. Strategic Praying
98. Strategy Of Warfare Praying
99. Stop Them Before They Stop You
100. Students In The School Of Fear
101. Symptoms Of Witchcraft Attack
102. The Baptism of Fire
103. The Battle Against The Spirit Of Impossibility
104. The Dinning Table Of Darkness
105. The Enemy Has Done This
106. The Evil Cry Of Your Family Idol
107. The Fire Of Revival
108. The Great Deliverance
109. The Internal Stumbling Block
110. The Lord Is A Man Of War
111. The Mystery Of Mobile Curses
112. The Mystery Of The Mobile Temple

113. The Prayer Eagle
114. The Power of Aggressive Prayer Warriors
115. The Pursuit Of Success
116. The Seasons Of Life
117. The Secrets Of Greatness
118. The Serpentine Enemies
119. The Skeleton In Your Grandfather's Cupboard
120. The Slow Learners
121. The Snake In The Power House
122. The Spirit Of The Crab
123. The star hunters
124. The Star In Your Sky
125. The Terrible Agenda
126. The Tongue Trap
127. The Unconquerable Power
128. The Unlimited God
129. The Vagabond Spirit
130. The Way Of Divine Encounter
131. The Wealth Transfer Agenda
132. Tied Down In The Spirits
133. Too Hot To Handle
134. Turnaround Breakthrough
135. Unprofitable Foundations
136. Vacancy For Mad Prophets
137. Victory Over Satanic Dreams
138. Victory Over Your Greatest Enemies
139. Violent Prayers Against Stubborn Situations
140. War At The Edge Of Breakthroughs

141. Wasting The Wasters
142. Wealth Must Change Hands
143. What You Must Know About The House Fellowship
144. When God Is Silent
145. When the Battle is from Home
146. When The Deliverer Need Deliverance
147. When Things Get Hard
148. When You Are Knocked Down
149. Where Is Your Faith
150. While Men Slept
151. Woman! Thou Art Loosed.
152. Your Battle And Your Strategy
153. Your Foundation And Destiny
154. Your Mouth And Your Deliverance

YORUBA PUBLICATIONS
1. ADURA AGBAYORI
2. ADURA TI NSI OKE NIDI
3. OJO ADURA

FRENCH PUBLICATIONS
1. PLUIE DE PRIERE
2. ESPIRIT DE VAGABONDAGE
3. EN FINIR AVEC LES FORCES MALEFIQUES DE LA MAISON DE TON PERE
4. QUE I'ENVOUTEMENT PERISSE
5. FRAPPEZ I'ADVERSAIRE ET IL FUIRA
6. COMMENT RECEVIOR LA DELIVRANCE DU MARI ET

FEMME DE NUIT
7. CPMMENT SE DELIVRER SOI-MEME
8. POVOIR CONTRE LES TERRORITES SPIRITUEL
9. PRIERE DE PERCEES POUR LES HOMMES D'AFFAIRES
10. PRIER JUSQU'A REMPORTER LA VICTOIRE
11. PRIERES VIOLENTES POUR HUMILIER LES PROBLEMES OPINIATRES
12. PRIERE POUR DETRUIRE LES MALADIES ET INFIRMITES
13. LE COMBAT SPIRITUEL ET LE FOYER
14. BILAN SPIRITUEL PERSONNEL
15. VICTOIRES SUR LES REVES SATANIQUES
16. PRIERES DE COMAT CONTRE 70 ESPIRITS DECHANINES
17. LA DEVIATION SATANIQUE DE LA RACE NOIRE
18. TON COMBAT ET TA STRATEGIE
19. VOTRE FONDEMENT ET VOTRE DESTIN
20. REVOQUER LES DECRETS MALEFIQUES
21. CANTIQUE DES CONTIQUES
22. LE MAUVAIS CRI DES IDOLES
23. QUAND LES CHOSES DEVIENNENT DIFFICILES
24. LES STRATEGIES DE PRIERES POUR LES CELIBATAIRES
25. SE LIBERER DES ALLIANCES MALEFIQUES
26. DEMANTELER LA SORCELLERIE
27. LA DELIVERANCE: LE FLACON DE MEDICAMENT DIEU
28. LA DELIVERANCE DE LA TETE
29. COMMANDER LE MATIN

30. NE GRAND MAIS LIE
31. POUVOIR CONTRE LES DEMOND TROPICAUX
32. LE PROGRAMME DE TRANFERT DE RICHESSE
33. LES ETUDIANTS A I'ECOLE DE LA PEUR
34. L'ETOILE DANS VOTRE CIEL
35. LES SAISONS DE LA VIE
36. FEMME TU ES LIBEREE

ANNUAL 70 DAYS PRAYER AND FASTING PUBLICATIONS

1. Prayers That Bring Miracles
2. Let God Answer By Fire
3. Prayers To Mount With Wings As Eagles
4. Prayers That Bring Explosive Increase
5. Prayers For Open Heavens
6. Prayers To Make You Fulfil Your Divine Destiny
7. Prayers That Make God To Answer And Fight By Fire
8. Prayers That Bring Unchallengeable Victory And Breakthrough Rainfall Bombardments
9. Prayers That Bring Dominion Prosperity And Uncommon Success
10. Prayers That Bring Power And Overflowing Progress
11. Prayers That Bring Laughter And Enlargement Breakthroughs
12. Prayers That Bring Uncommon Favour And Breakthroughs
13. Prayers That Bring Unprecedented Greatness & Unmatchable Increase
14. Prayers That Bring Awesome Testimonies And Turn Around Breakthroughs

www.ingramcontent.com/pod-product-compliance
Lightning Source LLC
Chambersburg PA
CBHW070755050426
42449CB00010B/2492